Life XP:

Unlocking Achievements and Leveling Up in the Real World

Charlcie Stinnett & Michelle Stinnett

Published by Charlcie Stinnett and Michelle Stinnett

Cover art and illustrations:
Cover design and illustrations by Charlcie Stinnett, courtesy of Midjourney.

Certain images and illustrations in this publication are in the public domain or are not subject to copyright. These images are used under the terms of the public domain or applicable copyright law and are not subject to the restrictions stated above. For specific information regarding the status of individual images or illustrations, please contact the publisher.

Print ISBN: 979-8-35094-885-1
eBook ISBN: 979-8-35094-886-8

Printed by BookBaby, a division of DIY Media Group

Disclaimer

This book, "Life XP: Unlocking Achievements and Leveling Up in the Real World," is intended for informational and educational purposes only. The authors, Charlcie Stinnett and Michelle Stinnett, are not licensed professionals in the fields of psychology, education, or any other specific discipline. The guidance, strategies, and information provided in this book are based on their personal experiences, research, and insights.

Readers are encouraged to consult with qualified professionals or experts in relevant fields when seeking personalized advice or assistance. The authors and the publisher disclaim any liability for the use or misuse of the information presented in this book. Individual results may vary, and success in real-life endeavors depends on various factors, including individual effort, circumstances, and external factors beyond the scope of this book.

Readers should exercise discretion and critical judgment when applying the principles and techniques discussed in this book to their own lives. It is the readers' responsibility to make informed decisions and seek appropriate guidance when necessary.

By reading this book, you acknowledge and accept the terms of this disclaimer.

Life XP:

Unlocking Achievements and Leveling Up in the Real World

Charlcie Stinnett & Michelle Stinnett

Table of Contents

About the Authors

Charlcie Stinnett holds a Bachelor's degree in Generalist Education, bringing a wealth of knowledge in teaching and learning strategies. Michelle Stinnett, with her Bachelor's degree in Psychology, adds a deep understanding of human behavior and motivation to the mix. As lifelong gamers and twins who share a passion for personal growth and gaming, their unique perspectives and experiences have come together to create "Life XP: Unlocking Achievements and Leveling Up in the Real World." Join them on this exciting journey where gaming meets personal development, and let their expertise guide you to success.

Introduction

Welcome to "Life XP: Unlocking Achievements and Leveling Up in the Real World," a book that invites you on an extraordinary journey—a journey that transcends the boundaries between the digital and real worlds. In the realm of video games, we've all experienced the thrill of embarking on epic quests, acquiring new skills, forming alliances, and overcoming formidable challenges. These adventures, while captivating in their own right, often serve as a source of inspiration and fascination for those seeking to enhance their lives beyond the screen.

Whether you're a dedicated gamer who spends hours immersed in virtual worlds, an anime enthusiast entranced by characters reborn in fantastical realms, or simply someone eager to unlock your full potential, this guide is tailored to your aspirations. Here, we unlock the treasure chest of wisdom hidden within the world of gaming and offer it to you as a blueprint for achieving your goals, gaining valuable experience, and continuously leveling up in your everyday life.

Within the pages of this guide, you will embark on a quest of self-discovery and personal growth. We will explore how to adopt the mindset of a gamer, setting clear objectives and embracing challenges as opportunities. You'll discover the power of determination and the drive to level up in every aspect of your life.

Just as in your favorite video games, you'll have the opportunity to shape your own character through the process of self-discovery, identifying your strengths, weaknesses, and interests. We'll discuss how to choose the right "class" for your real-life journey, be it a scholar, a warrior, a bard, or any other path you desire.

Effective goal setting is the cornerstone of progress, and we'll guide you on how to set SMART (Specific, Measurable, Achievable, Relevant, and Time-bound) goals and turn them into exciting quests. You'll learn how to break down big goals into manageable tasks and how to maintain motivation throughout your journey.

Imagine having a screen that displays your real-life experience points (XP), levels, and stats. In this guide, we'll reveal ways to track your progress and celebrate your achievements, providing the satisfaction of seeing your character grow. You'll discover how to use various tools and apps to gamify your life and make tracking your progress fun and engaging.

Unlocking new skills and abilities is a fundamental aspect of gaming, and we'll show you how to do it in real life. You'll explore effective methods for learning, from online courses and mentorship to self-directed practice. We'll delve into how to allocate skill points wisely to maximize your character's potential.

Life is filled with challenges and "boss battles," and we'll equip you with the strategies to approach these formidable foes with confidence, strategy, and teamwork. You'll learn problem-solving techniques and how to build a support network of allies to help you overcome obstacles.

Just as your character's health bar matters in the gaming world, we'll explore strategies for maintaining physical and mental well-being, including exercise, nutrition, and stress management. You'll discover how to harness the power of meditation and mindfulness to increase your vitality.

Building relationships and alliances can be the key to

success, just as in gaming. We'll discuss strategies for improving your social skills, networking effectively, and collaborating with others to achieve your goals. You'll learn how to build a party of like-minded individuals to tackle challenges together.

In the grand adventure of life, reaching the "end game" is a significant milestone. We'll help you define what success means to you and how to continue leveling up even after achieving your initial goals. You'll discover how to set new challenges and create a fulfilling and ever-evolving life.

Join us as we embark on this quest together, where the wisdom of gaming becomes a powerful tool for self-improvement and personal transformation. Whether you're a seasoned gamer or someone ready to embrace the principles of gaming for the first time, "Life XP: Unlocking Achievements and Leveling Up in the Real World" is your passport to a world of endless possibilities and achievements in the real world. Welcome to your new adventure—the adventure of a lifetime.

Chapter 1
The Gamer's Mindset

In the world of video games, success often hinges on more than just luck or innate skill; it's a matter of mindset. Gamers understand that their approach to each virtual challenge can make all the difference between victory and defeat. The good news is that this gamer's mindset can be a powerful tool in the real world as well. In this chapter, we'll dig deep into the core elements of the gamer's mindset and how you can use it to level up your real-life experiences.

Setting Clear Objectives

One of the first lessons you'll learn from gaming is the importance of setting clear objectives. In any game, whether it's completing a quest, defeating a boss, or achieving a high score, players know exactly what they need to do to succeed. This clarity of purpose guides their actions and decisions.

In real life, setting clear objectives can be equally powerful. Start by identifying what you want to achieve, whether it's advancing in your career, mastering a new skill, or improving your health. Make your goals specific, measurable, and achievable. By doing so, you create a roadmap for success, just as you would in a video game.

Embracing Challenges as Opportunities

Gamers thrive on challenges. They relish the chance to tackle difficult levels, puzzles, and foes. Challenges aren't seen as obstacles but rather as opportunities for growth and improvement. Every failure is a chance to learn, adapt, and ultimately overcome.

In real life, challenges are equally abundant. Instead of shying away from them, adopt the gamer's mentality of embracing these challenges as opportunities to level up. When faced with a difficult task or obstacle, see it as a chance to acquire new skills, gain experience, and become a more capable "character" in your own story.

Developing Resilience in the Face of Adversity

Gaming teaches us that setbacks are part of the journey. Gamers face defeat countless times, but they persist. This resilience is a hallmark of the gamer's mindset. They don't give up easily; they reload, respawn, and try again.

In your real life, you will encounter setbacks and failures. It's essential to develop the resilience to keep going despite these challenges. Remember that every time you overcome an adversity, you become stronger and more skilled, just like a character leveling up in a game.

The Power of Determination

Determination is a driving force in gaming. It's what keeps players glued to their screens, striving for that next achievement. Gamers understand that consistent effort and dedication pay off in the end. They don't expect instant success; they work for it.

In your real life, cultivating determination is crucial. Setbacks and obstacles will test your resolve, but with the gamer's mindset, you can stay focused on your goals and persevere. Whether you're aiming for career success, personal development, or any other achievement, remember that determination is your greatest ally.

The Drive to Level Up

At the heart of the gamer's mindset is the relentless drive to level up. Gamers are constantly seeking to improve their characters, acquire new skills, and reach higher levels of proficiency. This insatiable desire for progress is what keeps them engaged and motivated.

In your own life, this same drive can propel you to new heights. View every day as an opportunity to level up, to become a better version of yourself. Whether you're learning a new language, taking on a challenging project, or pursuing a fitness goal, maintain that innate gamer's hunger for improvement.

The gamer's mindset is a potent force that can transform the way you approach real-life challenges. By setting clear objectives, embracing challenges as opportunities, developing resilience, harnessing determination, and nurturing the drive to level up, you can unlock your full potential and achieve remarkable success in all aspects of your life. Just like your favorite video game characters, you too can embark on an epic journey of personal growth and triumph.

Chapter 2
Character Creation

In the world of video games, character creation is a pivotal moment. It's the point at which players define who they will become in the virtual world, shaping their abilities, appearance, and story. Remarkably, this concept can be applied to real life. In this chapter, we'll explore how you can craft your own character, much like in your favorite games, and embark on a real-life journey that aligns with your passions and ambitions.

Identifying Your Strengths

Every character in a game has strengths, and so do you. To create your real-life character, start by identifying your strengths. What are you naturally good at? What activities or skills come easily to you? These can be your unique abilities, your starting attributes.

Consider both tangible and intangible strengths. Are you physically strong, intellectually gifted, empathetic, or creative? These qualities can guide you toward your ideal character class in the game of life.

Acknowledging Your Weaknesses

No character in a game is without weaknesses, and the same goes for real life. It's essential to acknowledge your limitations and areas where you need improvement. Your weaknesses are not roadblocks but opportunities for growth.

Identifying your weaknesses allows you to work on them intentionally. Just as a character levels up by addressing their shortcomings, you can develop strategies to overcome your weaknesses and become a more well-rounded individual.

Exploring Your Interests

In video games, characters often choose their paths based on their interests and inclinations. Similarly, you can choose your real-life class by exploring your passions and interests. What activities make you lose track of time? What topics or hobbies ignite your enthusiasm?

Your interests can serve as a compass guiding you towards a fulfilling life. Whether it's a passion for science, sports, the arts, or any other field, these interests can help you define your character class in the real world.

Choosing Your Real-Life Class

Once you've identified your strengths, weaknesses, and interests, it's time to choose your real-life class. Think of this as selecting a character archetype that aligns with your character profile.

Are you drawn to the path of a scholar, thirsting for knowledge and intellectual growth? Perhaps the life of a warrior, where physical prowess and discipline are your focus, appeals to you. You might be inclined towards the path of a bard, where creativity and self-expression are your driving forces.

Remember that your class isn't set in stone; you can multiclass, just as characters in some games do. For instance, you might be a scholar by day and a bard by night. The key is to create a character class that resonates with your authentic self.

Choosing your class and character build:

-Create your character sheet and design your own real-life avatar.

-Assess your own abilities, talents, and interests to determine your character build.

-Identify your strengths, weaknesses, and skillsets.

-Understand the importance of specializing and focusing on your strengths.

-Develop strategies to improve weaknesses and turn them into strengths.

-Choose real-life skills to focus on and develop further.

-Establish your real-life goals and aspirations.

Character Classes

When creating your own character in real life, you can add an extra layer of fun and creativity by incorporating different classes that define your character's skills, abilities, and personality traits. Here are some class options for character creation:

Warrior:

As a warrior class, your character excels in physical prowess, strength, and combat-related skills. They might have expertise in marital arts, swordsmanship, or archery. Warriors thrive in competitive environments and enjoy challenges that push their physical limits.

Mage:

Mages possess extraordinary magical abilities and are skilled in spellcasting and manipulating arcane energies. They excel in intellectual pursuits, problem-solving, and strategic thinking. Mages are often seen as knowledgeable and wise characters with a penchant for mystical exploration.

Rogue:

Rogues are masters of stealth, agility, and dexterity. They possess exceptional skills in lock-picking. Rogues excel in sneaking around, gathering information discreetly, and executing precise and calculated actions.

Ranger:

Rangers have a deep connection with nature and possess exceptional survival skills. They excel in archery, tracking, and taming wild animals. Rangers are resourceful characters, who find solace and strength within the wilderness.

Bard:

Bards are charismatic and talented performers who captivate others with their music, storytelling, oratory skills, and charm. They excel in entertaining, inspiring, and persuading people. Bards are known for their creativity and the ability to adapt to various social situations.

Scholar:

Scholars are highly intelligent characters with a thirst for knowledge. They excel in research, studying ancient texts, and solving complex puzzles. Scholars possess a deep understanding of various subjects and are often sought after as advisors and experts in their field.

Healer:

Healers possess the ability to mend wounds, cure ailments, and provide support to their allies. They excel in the art of medicinal herbs, magical healing abilities, and nurturing others. Healers are compassionate and often prioritize the well-being of their companions.

Engineer:

Engineers are ingenious inventors and builders who excel in crafting, mechanical knowledge, and problem-solving. They have a knack for developing unique gadgets, powerful weapons, or intricate contraptions. Engineers bring practical solutions to complex challenges.

Tactician/Strategist:

Tacticians specialize in analyzing and planning battle strategies, utilizing their intelligence and leadership skills to gain an advantage on the battlefield. They are skilled in commanding and positioning their allies, optimizing their units' strengths while exploiting the weaknesses of their opponents. This class requires careful planning, strategic thinking, and foresight to excel. Players who enjoy analyzing situations and outsmarting their opponents will find this class appealing.

Let's embark on a journey to where you can take each of these character classes and apply them to the real world!

The Warrior

Positive Affirmation:

"I am a fearless and mighty warrior, ready to face any challenge with strength and skill!"

In real life, embodying the Warrior class can be interpreted as possessing physical strength, discipline, and a strong sense of determination. Here are some ways to incorporate the Warrior class into your everyday life.

19

1. Physical Fitness

As a Warrior, prioritize your physical well-being and engage in regular exercise. This can include strength training, martial arts, cardio workouts, or any physical activity that challenges and strengthens your body.

2. Self-Defense Training

Warriors excel in combat-related skills. Consider enrolling in self-defense classes or martial arts disciplines such as boxing, kickboxing, jiu-jitsu, or Krav Maga. These practices will not only enhance your physical abilities but also instill discipline and self-confidence.

3. Goal-setting and Discipline

Warriors are known for their focus, determination, and discipline. Set clear goals for yourself and create a structured routine to achieve them. Practice self-discipline by staying committed to your goals, whether they are related to fitness, career, personal growth, or any other aspect of your life.

4. Competitive Spirit

Warriors thrive in competitive environments. Challenge yourself by participating in sports or other competitive activities that push your limits and help you develop a mindset of taking calculated risks and overcoming obstacles.

5. Mental Resilience

A Warrior possesses mental resilience and grit. Cultivate mental strength by practicing mindfulness and resilience-building exercises. This can include meditation, visualization, affirmations, and reflection to develop a calm and focused mindset.

6. Leadership Skills

Warriors often take on leadership roles and rally others for a cause. Enhance your leadership skills by taking charge of situations, making informed decisions, and inspiring others through your actions and words.

7. Positive Mindset

Warriors remain optimistic even in difficult situations. Cultivate a positive mindset by practicing gratitude, focusing on self-improvement, and surrounding yourself with supportive and positive influences.

Remember, incorporating the Warrior class into your real-life avatar is about embracing the traits and skills associated with warriors, rather than engaging in actual physical combat. It's a symbolic representation of your determination, discipline, and strength in overcoming challenges and achieving personal growth.

The Mage

Positive Affirmation:

"I am a powerful mage, a master of magic and wisdom, capable of harnessing the elements to overcome any obstacle!"

In real life, embodying the Mage class can be interpreted as possessing intellectual prowess, curiosity, and a strong connection to knowledge and magic/energy. Here are some ways to incorporate the Mage class into your everyday life.

1. Lifelong Learning

Mages are known for their thirst for knowledge. Embrace a lifelong learning approach by constantly seeking new information and expanding your understanding of various subjects. Read books, take online courses, attend lectures, and engage in intellectual conversations to broaden your horizons.

2. Intellectual Pursuits

Mages excel in intellectual pursuits such as problem-solving, critical thinking, and creativity. Engage in activities that stimulate your mind, such as solving puzzles, playing strategy games, solving riddles, or participating in brainstorming sessions to exercise your cognitive abilities.

3. Magic Practices

You can explore practices that connect to the concept of magic. This can include meditation, visualization techniques, energy work, tarot reading, astrology, or any other spiritual or metaphysical practice that resonates with you.

4. Creative Expression

Mages often possess a creative side. Nurture your creativity by engaging in artistic endeavors such as painting, writing, music, or any other form of self-expression that resonates with you. Allow your imagination to soar and explore different ways to channel your creativity into tangible forms.

5. Seek Wisdom

Mages are known for seeking wisdom from various sources. Engage in philosophical discussions, seek guidance from mentors or wise individuals in your field, and actively seek perspectives different from your own. Always be open to learning from others and seeking wisdom from diverse sources.

6. Problem-Solving and Innovation

Mages are skilled problem solvers and innovators. Channel your intellect and creativity into finding solutions to challenges or coming up with new ideas. Cultivate an innovative mindset and always be on the lookout for ways to improve upon existing systems or create something new.

Remember, adopting the Mage class in real life is about embracing the attributes and skills associated with mages. It's a symbolic representation of your intellectual curiosity, thirst for knowledge, and creative problem-solving abilities.

The Rogue

Positive Affirmation:

"I am a cunning and agile rogue, a master of stealth and quick thinking. I embrace the shadows and outwit my enemies with finesse and precision!"

In real life, embodying the Rogue class can be interpreted as possessing characteristics such as agility, stealth, adaptability, and resourcefulness. Here are some ways to incorporate the Rogue class into your everyday life.

1. Cultivate Physical Agility:

Rogues are known for their physical dexterity and agility. Engage in activities that promote physical fitness and enhance your coordination, balance, and flexibility. Consider practicing marital arts, parkour, dance, yoga, or any other activity that challenges your physical abilities.

2. Develop Stealth and Observation Skills

Rogues excel in being discreet and observant. Practice mindfulness and improve your ability to observe details in your surroundings. Practice stealthy movements and develop a keen eye for spotting patterns or anomalies. This can also be applied to problem-solving situations, where observing subtle cues can lead to finding creative solutions.

3. Master the Art of Adaptability

Rogues are adaptable and quick to adjust to different situations. Work on developing your ability to adapt to new circumstances, be open to change, and be willing to take calculated risks. Embrace new experiences, step out of your comfort zone, and learn to thrive in unpredictable environments.

4. Learn Practical Skills

Rogues are often skilled in various practical abilities. Develop skills that are useful in everyday life, such as cooking, first aid, outdoor survival skills, lockpicking (as a hobby and with proper permissions), or any other practical skill that can come in handy in different situations.

5. Networking and Social Skills

Rogues are often charismatic and skilled in social interaction. Work on developing your networking and communication skills to navigate social situations with ease. Learn to read people, build rapport, and adapt your communication style to different individuals and contexts.

6. Problem-Solving and Critical Thinking

Rogues are known for their ability to think on their feet and solve problems quickly. Hone your critical thinking skills and practice solving puzzles, riddles, or brain teasers. Cultivate an analytical mindset and develop your decision-making abilities to approach challenges from different angles.

7. Embrace Resourcefulness

Rogues rely on their resourcefulness to get things done. Foster a mindset of finding creative solutions with limited resources. Look for unconventional approaches, think outside the box, and develop the ability to improvise when faced with unexpected obstacles.

Remember, adopting the Rogue class in real life is about embracing the attributes and skills associated with rogues, rather than engaging in illegal or harmful activities. It's a symbolic representation of your ability to adapt, think quickly, and be resourceful in various aspects of life.

The Ranger

Positive Affirmation:

"I am a skilled ranger, connected to the natural world and skilled with both bow and blade. I am one with the wilderness, and my aim is true!"

Embodying the Ranger class in real life involves adopting qualities such as being connected to nature, having wilderness survival skills, being a skilled tracker, and having a deep respect for the environment. Here are some ways to incorporate the Ranger class into your everyday life.

1. Connect with Nature

Spending time in nature is crucial for a Ranger. Make it a priority to spend time outdoors regularly. Explore local parks, forests, or nature reserves. Hike, camp, or go on nature walks to immerse yourself in the natural world. This will help you develop a connection with the environment and appreciate its beauty.

2. Learn Wilderness Survival Skills

Rangers are adept at surviving in the wild. Learn essential wilderness survival skills such as fire building, shelter construction, identifying edible plants, navigation using maps and compasses, and basic first aid. Take survival courses or find educational resources to further your knowledge.

3. Study Tracking and Wildlife Observation

Rangers are skilled in tracking animals and observing wildlife. Familiarize yourself with tracking techniques, such as identifying animal footprints, scat, feeding signs, and other clues left by wildlife. Learn about local ecosystems, types of flora and fauna, and how they interact.

4. Practice Archery or Marksmanship

Rangers are often skilled marksmen. Consider taking up archery, target shooting, or other forms of marksmanship. Join a local archery club or find a shooting range to practice your skills. Remember to prioritize safety and adhere to all rules and regulations.

5. Become an Environmental Steward

Rangers have a deep respect for the environment and actively work to protect it. Volunteer for local conservation organizations, participate in clean-up initiatives, or get involved in campaigns that promote environmental sustainability. Help raise awareness about ecological issues and inspire others to take action.

6. Cultivate Wilderness Awareness

Rangers have a keen sense of their surroundings and are attuned to the wilderness. Develop your observation and awareness skills by practicing mindfulness in nature. Pay attention to sounds, smells, textures, and colors in the environment. Practice deep listening and experience the beauty of the natural world around you.

7. Learn Bushcraft Skills

Rangers are adept at utilizing natural resources for survival. Learn bushcraft skills such as foraging for wild edible plants, making simple tools from natural materials, building natural shelters, and purifying water. These skills will enhance your self-reliance in the wilderness.

Remember, adopting the Ranger class in real life involves cultivating a deep connection with nature, developing wilderness skills, and becoming an advocate for the environment. The goal is to develop a sense of harmony with the natural world and inspire others to appreciate and protect it.

The Bard

Positive Affirmation:

"I am a charismatic bard, captivating audiences with my music and words. My melodies inspire courage and my tales weave magic. I bring joy and inspiration wherever I go!"

Embodying the Bard class in real life involves embracing qualities such as creativity, charisma, musicality, and storytelling. Bards are known for their ability to entertain, inspire, and captivate audiences. Here are some ways to incorporate the Bard class into your everyday life.

1. Develop Musical Skills

Bards are known for their musical talents. Learn to play an instrument, whether it's a guitar, piano, flute, or any other instrument that resonates with you. Take lessons, join a local music group, or learn through online tutorials. Practice regularly to improve your skills and expand your repertoire.

2. Cultivate Artistic Expression

Bards are creative individuals. Explore various forms of artistic expression, such as painting, drawing, writing, or dancing. Find a medium that speaks to you and allows you to express yourself. Attend art classes, workshops, or join a local art group to further develop your artistic abilities.

3. Tell Stories and Perform

Bards are natural storytellers. Hone your storytelling skills by practicing the art of oral storytelling. Learn different narrative techniques, practice voice modulation, and engage your audience through captivating tales. Consider joining a local storytelling group or performing at open mic events.

4. Improve Communication and Charisma

Bards are charismatic and skilled communicators. Work on improving your interpersonal skills by participating in activities that involve public speaking or acting. Take communication courses, join a local theater group, or engage in activities that boost your confidence and charisma.

5. Support Local Arts and Culture

Bards often foster a sense of community through their performances and support for the arts. Attend local theater productions, music concerts, poetry readings, and other cultural events. Show your support by purchasing artwork, supporting local artists, and spreading the word about their work.

6. Embrace Emotional Intelligence

Bards have a deep understanding of emotions and use them to connect with others. Cultivate emotional intelligence by practicing active listening, empathy, and understanding. Foster meaningful connections with those around you and use your emotional intelligence to inspire and uplift others.

7. Spread Positivity and Inspiration

Bards have the power to inspire and uplift others through their performances and presence. Use your talents and creativity to spread positivity, share stories, and uplift those around you. Consider starting a blog or social media page where you can share your art, stories, and other inspiring content.

Remember, embodying the Bard class in real life means embracing creativity, captivating storytelling, and using your skills to inspire and entertain others. The goal is to create a rich and vibrant world through music, art, and storytelling, while fostering connections with others.

The Scholar

Positive Affirmation:

"I am a knowledgeable scholar, constantly seeking to expand my mind and uncover the secrets of the world. My intellect is a powerful tool, and I embrace the pursuit of wisdom!"

Embodying the Scholar class in real life involves embracing qualities such as knowledge, curiosity, critical thinking, and a thirst for learning. Scholars are known for their expertise in a particular field and their dedication to expanding their knowledge. Here are some ways to incorporate the Scholar class into your everyday life.

1. Choose an Area of Study

Scholars specialize in a specific field of knowledge. Find an area of interest that fascinates you, whether it's history, science, literature, philosophy, psychology, or any other subject. Dedicate time to studying and researching that field, seeking out reliable sources and expanding your knowledge.

2. Pursue Higher Education

Scholars often pursue advanced degrees to deepen their understanding of their chosen field. Consider enrolling in university or college programs that align with your area of interest. Take advantage of online courses, workshops, and seminars to continue your education.

3. Develop Critical Thinking Skills

Scholars rely on critical thinking to analyze and evaluate information. Work on developing your critical thinking skills by questioning assumptions, seeking multiple perspectives, and recognizing biases. Read books and articles that challenge your beliefs and engage in intellectual discussions with others.

4. Write and Publish

Scholars often contribute to their field by writing and publishing research papers or books. Practice writing regularly by starting a blog, contributing to articles in magazines or journals, or even writing a book. Share your knowledge and insights with others, while seeking feedback to improve your writing.

5. Attend Conferences and Workshops

Scholars engage in academic communities by attending conferences, workshops, and seminars. Look for conferences or events in your field of interest where you can network with fellow experts, learn from others, and share your own research or insights.

6. Be a Lifelong Learner

Scholars have a deep commitment to lifelong learning. Embrace a growth mindset and actively seek out new knowledge and skills. Engage in self-study, take online courses, participate in webinars, and attend lectures or talks by experts in your field.

7. Share knowledge

Scholars often find fulfillment in sharing their knowledge with others. Consider becoming a mentor or tutor to aspiring learners in your field. Volunteer to teach or present at educational institutions, community centers, or local organizations.

Remember, embodying the Scholar class in real life means embracing a love for learning, seeking knowledge, and becoming an expert in a particular field. Continuously challenge yourself and stay curious as you immerse yourself in the profound aspects of your preferred subject. Share your insights and contribute to the intellectual development of your community.

The Healer

Positive Affirmation:

"I am a compassionate healer, restoring health and reviving hope. My hands radiate soothing energy, and I am a beacon of support for my allies in their darkest moments!"

Embodying the Healer class in real life involves nurturing and caring for others, whether it's through physical healing, emotional support, or spiritual guidance. Healers are known for their compassion, empathy, and healing abilities. Here are some ways to incorporate the Healer class into your everyday life.

1. Develop Empathy

Healers excel in understanding the emotions and experiences of others. Practice empathizing with others by actively listening, trying to put yourself in their shoes, and offering support and validation. Cultivate compassion and understanding towards those around you.

2. Acquire First Aid and Medical Skills

Healers are often skilled in first aid and medical techniques. Consider taking first aid and CPR courses to learn essential life-saving skills. Explore opportunities to deepen your medical knowledge by volunteering at hospitals, clinics, or healthcare facilities.

3. Provide Emotional Support

Healers offer emotional support and a compassionate ear to those in need. Be an empathetic listener for others, offering a safe space for them to express their thoughts and feelings. Learn active listening techniques and practice holding space for others without judgment.

4. Promote Health and Wellness

Healers prioritize preventive care and wellness. Focus on maintaining your own physical and mental health through regular exercise, a balanced diet, and self-care. Encourage others to take care of their well-being by sharing tips, resources, and leading by example.

5. Study Complementary Therapies

Healers often explore alternative and complementary therapies to support healing. Consider studying practices such as massage therapy, acupuncture, Reiki, herbal medicine, aromatherapy, or other holistic modalities. Seek out reputable training programs to gain the necessary knowledge and skills.

6. Cultivate a Healing Presence

Healers often possess a calming and nurturing presence that promotes healing. Practice mindfulness and cultivate a peaceful demeanor. Be a source of support and comfort for those around you, offering gentle encouragement and reassurance.

Remember, embodying the Healer class in real life means embracing compassion, empathy, and a commitment to helping others. Strive to make a positive impact in people's lives, whether it's through physical healing, emotional support, or spiritual guidance. Listen actively, learn therapeutic techniques, and promote wellness in both yourself and in others.

The Engineer

Positive Affirmation:

"I am a brilliant engineer, crafting solutions with my innovative mind and deft hands. I build, repair, and modify with precision, ensuring nothing is beyond my grasp. My creations shape the world around me!"

Embodying the Engineer class in real life involves taking on the role of a problem solver, builder, and innovator. Engineers are known for their technical skills, logical thinking, and ability to design and create solutions. Here are some ways to incorporate the Engineer class into your everyday life.

1. Develop Technical Skills

Engineers are highly skilled in a specific area of expertise, such as mechanical, civil, or electrical engineering. Identify your interests and pursue education or training in that field. Develop technical skills through courses, certifications, or hands-on projects.

2. Embrace Analytical Thinking

Engineers are logical and analytical thinkers. Cultivate your problem-solving abilities by approaching challenges with a systematic and structured mindset. Break complex problems into smaller, more manageable parts and analyze them to identify potential solutions.

3. Create and Innovate

Engineers are often involved in designing and creating new solutions. Embrace your creativity and curiosity by exploring innovative ideas. Engage in DIY projects, build prototypes, or experiment with new technologies that align with your interests.

4. Collaborate in a Team

Engineers often work in collaborative environments where teamwork is essential. Hone your communication and collaboration skills by actively participating in group projects or joining professional organizations related to your field of interest.

5. Continuous Learning

Engineering is a constantly evolving field, and engineers need to stay updated with the latest developments and technologies. Commit to lifelong learning by staying curious and seeking out opportunities to expand your knowledge and skills.

6. Attention to Detail

Engineers pay close attention to details to ensure the accuracy and quality of their work. Cultivate a mindset of precision and thoroughness in your everyday tasks, whether it's in your personal projects or professional responsibilities.

Remember, embodying the Engineer class in real life means developing technical skills, embracing analytical thinking, and being a creative problem solver. Stay curious, continuously learn and adapt to new technologies, collaborate with others, and adhere to ethical standards. By applying engineering principles in your everyday life, you can become a skilled problem solver and contribute to building a better world.

The Tactician/Strategist

Positive Affirmation:

"I am a strategic tactician, analyzing every angle and anticipating every move. My mind is a weapon honed for battle, and I lead my allies with precision and insight. Victory is within reach with my brilliant strategies!"

Embodying the Tactician/Strategist class in real life involves cultivating certain characteristics and pursuing relevant experiences and knowledge. Here are some ways to incorporate the Tactician/Strategist class into your everyday life.

1. Analytical and Critical thinking skills

A Tactician/Strategist class must possess strong analytical and critical thinking skills. This involves the ability to assess complex situations, break them down into smaller components, and identify patterns and connections between them. Developing this skill can be accomplished through formal education, such as studying fields like military strategy, business management, or political science. Reading books on these subjects or studying real-life examples of successful strategists can also help cultivate this skill.

2. Decision Making Abilities

Another important aspect of being a Tactician/ Strategist class is excellent decision-making abilities. This includes being able to gather information, evaluate potential options, weigh the risks and benefits, and make informed choices under pressure. Developing this skill can be done through practice, by taking on leadership roles that require making decisions, as well as learning from both successes and failures.

3. Communication Skills

Effective communication skills are essential for a Tactician/Strategist class, as they need to convey their plans and ideas clearly to others. This involves being able to articulate complex concepts concisely, listen actively, and collaborate with a team. Improving communication skills can be achieved through practice, seeking feedback, and participating in activities that require effective communication, such as public speaking or group projects.

4. Organizational and Time-Management Skills

A Tactician/Strategist class should also possess strong organizational and time management skills. Keeping track of multiple tasks and priorities, developing long-term plans, and juggling various responsibilities are crucial elements of this class. Developing organizational skills can be accomplished through techniques such as creating schedules, setting goals, and breaking down complex tasks into manageable steps.

5. Adaptability and Creative Thinking

A Tactician/Strategist class requires adaptability and the ability to think creatively. This involves being open to new ideas, considering alternate approaches, and finding innovative solutions to problems. Cultivating creativity can be done through activities such as brainstorming, exploring different perspectives, and engaging in creative hobbies.

Remember, embodying the Tactician/Strategist class in real life means striving to develop and embody the skills and traits associated with this class. Work towards becoming an effective strategist and leader in various fields such as military, business, politics, and more.

Developing Your Character Sheet

In the gaming world, characters have character sheets that detail their attributes, skills, and abilities. Similarly, you can create a real-life character sheet. List your strengths, weaknesses, interests, and chosen class. This character sheet will serve as a reference point for your real-life journey.

Refer to your character sheet regularly as a reminder of who you are and who you aspire to become. It will help you make decisions that align with your character's goals and values, just as a player makes choices for their in-game character.

Character creation in the real world is a dynamic process, much like crafting a video game character. By identifying your strengths, acknowledging your weaknesses, exploring your interests, and choosing a real-life class that resonates with your passions, you can embark on a journey that aligns with your authentic self. Just as in your favorite games, your character's story is in your hands, and the possibilities for growth and fulfillment are boundless.

Character Creation

In the world of gaming and personal development, your character represents you—your strengths, weaknesses, and unique attributes. Just as in your favorite video games, creating a well-defined character profile is the first step towards your real-life adventure. Use these pages to craft your character for the journey ahead.

Character Name:

_____

_____

Character Class:

_____

_____

Class Description (Include your chosen class's strengths and weaknesses):

Character Attributes:

Strengths:

List your key strengths, talents, and skills. What are you naturally good at? What sets you apart from others?

Strength 1:

_____

_____

Strength 2:

_____

_____

Strength 3:

_____

_____

Weaknesses:

Acknowledge your areas for improvement or weaknesses that may challenge you in your journey.

Weakness 1:

_____

_____

Weakness 2:

_____

_____

Weakness 3:

_____

_____

Character Backstory:

Every character has a backstory—a history that defines who they are. What experiences, challenges, or pivotal moments have shaped you?

_____

_____

_____

_____

_____

Character Goals:

Define your character's goals and aspirations for this real-life adventure. What are you striving to achieve, and what motivates you?

Short-term Goal (within the next year):

_____

_____

Mid-term Goal (within the next 1-5 years):

_____

_____

Long-term Goal (5+ years):

_____

_____

Character Alignment:

Consider your character's alignment—a reflection of your moral and ethical compass. Are you more aligned with being good, neutral, or leaning towards the chaotic?

Alignment:

_____

Character Appearance:

Your character's appearance can influence how others perceive you. Describe your character's physical attributes, style, and any distinguishing features.

_____

_____

_____

_____

Draw Your Character

Character Gear and Equipment:

In gaming, gear and equipment can enhance your abilities. In real life, these represent the tools, resources, and knowledge you possess.

List some of your character's "gear" and resources that can help you on your journey.

Gear/Resource 1:

_____

Gear/Resource 2:

_____

Gear/Resource 3:

_____

Character Allies and Supporters:

No character succeeds alone. Who are your allies and supporters—friends, mentors, or individuals who contribute to your journey?

Ally/Supporter 1:

_____

Ally/Supporter 2:

_____

Ally/Supporter 3:

_____

Character Quote:

Choose or create a motivating quote that encapsulates your character's philosophy or outlook on life.

Character Quote:

_____

_____

_____

Your character profile is a living document that can evolve and adapt as you progress through your real-life adventure. Take the time to reflect on your character and revisit this page whenever you need to recalibrate your path or set new goals. Remember, your character is a reflection of your potential, and you have the power to shape your own narrative in the grand adventure of life.

Chapter 3
Gamify Your Progress with Real-Life Stats

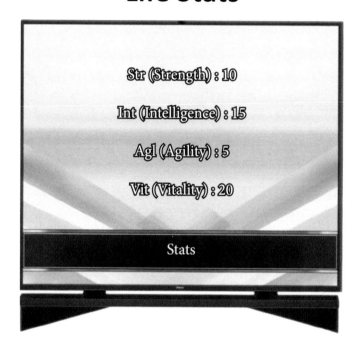

In the world of gaming, numbers matter. Your character's stats, such as strength, vitality, agility, and intelligence, play a vital role in determining your success. What if you could apply this gamification principle to your real-life journey of personal growth and self-improvement? In this chapter, we'll explore how to measure subjective stats by earning points in real life, turning your everyday activities into exciting adventures.

The Power of Points

Measuring your real-life stats with a point system can be both fun and motivating. Just like in your favorite RPG, you'll gain experience points (XP) and level up your character—yourself. Let's explore the process.

Establish a Point System

The first step is to create a point system where you assign values to different activities or achievements related to each stat. Think of this as defining the rules of your personal game. Consider assigning points for completing specific workouts, practicing mindfulness, solving puzzles, or even reading educational books. For each activity, determine how many points it's worth.

Set Goals

To level up effectively, you need goals. Set specific and challenging goals for each stat. Your strength goal might involve increasing the weight you can lift, while your agility goal could focus on improving your performance in a particular physical skill. Define your goals to keep your journey focused and exciting.

Track Your Activities

To earn points, you must keep a record of your activities. This can be done through a journal, a spreadsheet, or a mobile app designed for tracking goals and achievements. Each time you complete an activity, record it along with the points you've earned. This record will become your personal achievement log.

Calculate Points

Assign points to each activity based on its difficulty or the effort required. For instance, lifting heavier weights or mastering complex agility drills should yield more points than easier tasks. Be consistent in your point assignment and update it as you progress and your abilities improve.

Monitor Your Progress

Regularly review your points and track your progress toward your goals. The act of monitoring your stats can be highly motivating, much like watching your character's level increase in a game. This process allows you to see how far you've come and helps you stay on course.

Celebrate Achievements

When you reach a milestone or achieve a goal, celebrate your accomplishment. Rewards can be as simple as treating yourself to a favorite meal or acknowledging your hard work and dedication. Celebrating achievements reinforces the sense of accomplishment and motivates you to reach new heights.

Let's take a look at an example of a fun and gaming-inspired point system for strength, vitality, intelligence, and agility in real life:

Strength Points (STR):

- Earn 10 points for completing a challenging workout session.

- Gain 5 points for reaching a new personal record in weightlifting or bodyweight exercises.

- Receive 15 points for participating in a team sport or completing a physically demanding task.

Vitality Points (VIT):

- Accumulate 10 points for getting a full night's rest (7-9 hours).

- Earn 15 points for preparing and eating a healthy, balanced meal.

- Gain 5 points for completing a mindfulness or meditation session.

Intelligence Points (INT):

- Earn 15 points for reading a non-fiction book or completing an educational course/workshop.

- Gain 10 points for solving a challenging puzzle or brainteaser.

- Receive 5 points for actively learning something new through research.

Agility Points (AGL):

- Accumulate 15 points for learning or mastering a new physical skill like dancing, martial arts, or parkour.

- Earn 10 points for participating in a fast-paced sport or game that requires quick reflexes.

- Gain 5 points for completing a flexibility or coordination-based workout routine.

Additionally, consider setting milestones to unlock special rewards as you accumulate points in each category. For example, reaching 50 points in Strength could award you with new workout gear, or reaching 50 points in Intelligence could grant you a book of your choice.

Remember, the primary goal of this point system is to gamify your personal growth journey. It adds an element of fun and motivation to your daily activities. While the numbers matter, don't lose sight of the overall improvement and positive changes you experience in your life. Your character is leveling up, and your real-life adventure has just begun. So, keep earning those points and embrace the journey!

Gamify Your Progress with Real-Life Stats: Activity Log

Character Stats:

- **Strength (STR):** _____ points

- **Vitality (VIT):** _____ points

- **Intelligence (INT):** _____ points

- **Agility (AGL):** _____ points

Establish Your Point System:

Create a point system by assigning values to activities related to each stat. Be creative and make it your own!

Strength (STR) Activities:

Activity 1:

_____

_____

Points: _____

Activity 2:

_____

_____

Points: _____

Activity 3:

_____

_____

Points: _____

Vitality (VIT) Activities:

Activity 1:

_____

_____

Points: _____

Activity 2:

_____

_____

Points: _____

Activity 3:

_____

_____

Points: _____

Intelligence (INT) Activities:

Activity 1:

_____

_____

Points: _____

Activity 2:

_____

_____

Points: _____

Activity 3:

_____

_____

Points: _____

Agility (AGL) Activities:

Activity 1:

_____

_____

Points: _____

Activity 2:

_____

_____

Points: _____

Activity 3:

_____

_____

Points: _____

Goals:

Set specific goals for each stat. What are you striving to achieve?

Strength (STR) Goal:

_____

_____

Vitality (VIT) Goal:

_____

_____

Intelligence (INT) Goal:

_____

_____

Agility (AGL) Goal:

_____

_____

Progress Tracking:

Keep a record of your activities and points earned in your journey toward leveling up.

Date: _____

Activity:

_____

_____

Points Earned: _____

Date: _____

Activity:

_____

_____

Points Earned: _____

Date: _____

Activity:

_____

_____

Points Earned: _____

Milestones and Rewards:

Consider setting milestones to unlock special rewards as you accumulate points. What rewards motivate you?

Strength (STR) Milestone Reward:

_____

_____

Vitality (VIT) Milestone Reward:

_____

_____

Intelligence (INT) Milestone Reward:

_____

_____

Agility (AGL) Milestone Reward:

_____

_____

Notes:

Use this space to jot down any thoughts, ideas, or reflections on your gamified journey.

_____

_____

_____

_____

_____

_____

Remember, these pages are your personal character sheets in the grand adventure of life. Keep it updated, set your goals high, and enjoy leveling up your real-life stats!

Chapter 4
XP and Progress Tracking

In the world of video games, the constant feedback of experience points (XP), levels, and stats is a driving force that keeps players engaged and motivated. But what if you could bring this gamified approach to your real life? In this chapter, we'll explore the concept of XP and progress tracking outside the gaming world and how it can provide a tangible and rewarding way to monitor your journey of personal growth and achievement.

The Power of Real-Life XP

Imagine if every achievement, big or small, earned you experience points that contributed to your character's growth in the game of life. While we can't display this on a screen like in a video game, we can certainly adopt the idea of earning real-life XP.

Start by assigning values or XP to your goals, tasks, and accomplishments. For example, completing a challenging project at work might earn you 1000 XP, while spending an hour practicing a new skill could be worth 50 XP. This numerical representation of your progress adds a layer of gamification to your real-life journey, making it more engaging and satisfying.

Tracking Your Progress

In video games, players have access to detailed stats and progress tracking tools. In real life, you can use various methods and tools to monitor your progress:

Journaling

Keep a journal or digital diary to record your daily achievements, challenges, and personal growth. This serves as a record of your journey and allows you to reflect on your experiences.

Goal Tracking Apps

Numerous apps are designed to help you set and track your goals. These apps often include features like progress bars, reminders, and notifications to keep you on track.

Spreadsheets

Create a spreadsheet to track your goals, XP earned, and levels achieved. This visual representation allows you to see your progress over time and can be highly motivating.

Online Communities

Join online communities or forums where members share their goals and progress. These communities provide support, accountability, and inspiration.

Reward Systems

Implement a reward system where reaching certain XP milestones results in real-life rewards, such as a special treat, a day off, or a small purchase.

Celebrating Your Achievements

Just as video games celebrate achievements with fanfare and rewards, it's essential to celebrate your real-life successes. Acknowledge your milestones, whether they are significant accomplishments or small victories. Celebration reinforces your motivation and provides a sense of accomplishment.

Create your own celebration rituals, such as treating yourself to a favorite meal, sharing your success with friends and family, or taking a moment of reflection to appreciate your journey. The act of celebration not only boosts your morale but also encourages you to keep moving forward.

Gamifying Your Life

To make tracking your progress even more engaging, consider gamifying your life. Set challenges, quests, and mini games for yourself. For example, if you're learning a new language, challenge yourself to have a 10-minute conversation with a native speaker or complete a daily vocabulary quiz.

Apps and tools designed for gamification can also help. Some apps turn habit-building into a game where you earn rewards or points for consistent behavior, making it more enjoyable to establish positive habits.

The Satisfaction of Character Growth

In video games, seeing your character grow and improve is immensely satisfying. In real life, tracking your progress and earning XP can provide the same sense of achievement and growth. By adopting these gamification techniques, you can turn your real-life journey into an exciting adventure where every step forward brings you closer to becoming the best version of yourself.

The concept of XP and progress tracking from the gaming world can be a powerful tool for personal development and motivation in real life. By assigning values to your achievements, tracking your progress through various methods and tools, celebrating your successes, and gamifying your life, you can make your journey more engaging, satisfying, and rewarding. Just like a skilled gamer, you have the ability to level up and grow as you navigate the challenges and adventures of your own life.

Tracking XP (Experience Points)

In the world of gaming, experience points (XP) represent your progress and growth. Use these pages to track your real-life XP and celebrate your achievements, just as you would in your favorite video game.

XP Log:

Record your XP earned from various real-life achievements, milestones, and quests. Assign a value to each achievement based on its significance and impact on your personal growth.

Achievement/Milestone:

_____

_____

XP Earned: _____

Achievement/Milestone:

_____

_____

XP Earned: _____

Achievement/Milestone:

_____

_____

XP Earned: _____

Achievement/Milestone:

_____

_____

XP Earned: _____

Achievement/Milestone:

_____

_____

XP Earned: _____

Total XP Earned: _____

Level Progress:

Determine your character's level based on your total XP. Use the following table to identify your level and set goals for reaching the next one.

Level 1: _____

Level 2: _____

Level 3: _____

Level 4: _____

Level 5: _____

Level 6: _____

Level 7: _____

Level 8: _____

Level 9: _____

Level 10: _____

Rewards and Abilities Unlocked:

List any rewards or abilities you've unlocked as you level up. These could be personal achievements, skills acquired, or new opportunities.

Reward/Ability:

_____

_____

Unlocked at Level: _____

Reward/Ability:

_____

_____

Unlocked at Level: _____

Reward/Ability:

_____

_____

Unlocked at Level: _____

Progress Tracking

Tracking your progress is crucial for staying on course and maintaining motivation. Use this to monitor your journey's advancement, set new goals, and celebrate your accomplishments.

Current Goal:

_____

_____

Progress Updates:

Document your progress toward your current goal. Include details about tasks completed, milestones reached, and challenges overcome.

Progress Update:

_____

_____

Progress Update:

_____

_____

Progress Update:

_____

_____

Progress Update:

_____

_____

Progress Update:

_____

_____

Next Steps:

Identify the next steps you need to take to move closer to your goal. What tasks or actions will you focus on in the upcoming weeks or months?

Next Step:

_____

_____

Next Step:

_____

_____

Next Step:

_____

_____

Next Step:

_____

_____

Next Step:

_____

_____

Goal Completion:

Once you've achieved your goal, celebrate your success and consider setting a new one. Describe how achieving this goal has impacted your character's journey.

Goal Completed:

_____

_____

Impact on Character's Journey:

_____

_____

_____

_____

These XP and Progress Tracking pages will help you monitor your real-life progress and celebrate your achievements along your journey. Just like in gaming, leveling up and tracking your character's growth can be a motivating and rewarding experience in your everyday life.

Chapter 5
Setting Goals and Quests

In the realm of video games, objectives are crystal clear, and progress is often tracked meticulously. Much like a gamer navigating a virtual world, setting and achieving real-life goals requires strategy, focus, and determination. In this chapter, we'll delve into the art of setting goals and transforming them into exciting quests that propel you towards success. We'll also explore techniques to maintain motivation as you embark on your real-life journey.

Understanding the Importance of Effective Goal Setting

Goal setting is the foundation of progress in both gaming and real life. Just as a gamer needs a clear objective to advance in the game, you need well-defined goals to move forward in your personal and professional endeavors.

Effective goal setting involves creating goals that are **SMART**:

Specific

Your goals should be clear and precise. Avoid vague objectives and define precisely what you want to achieve.

Measurable

Goals should have quantifiable metrics to track your progress. How will you know when you've accomplished them?

Achievable

Goals should be realistic and attainable. They should challenge you but still be within your reach.

Relevant

Your goals should align with your character, interests, and aspirations. They should be meaningful and relevant to your life.

Time-bound

Set a specific timeframe for achieving your goals. This creates a sense of urgency and helps you stay on track.

Transforming Goals into Quests

To make your goals more engaging and motivating, consider reframing them as quests. In video games, quests are exciting missions that characters undertake to achieve rewards and progress the storyline. Similarly, transforming your goals into quests can make your real-life journey more compelling.

For example, if your goal is to lose weight, turn it into a quest like "The Fitness Challenge." Give it a backstory, such as "You are a warrior on a quest to improve your health and fitness." Assign rewards for completing milestones along the way, just like earning experience points and loot in a game. This gamified approach can make pursuing your goals more exciting and enjoyable.

Breaking Down Big Goals into Manageable Tasks

In video games, players often tackle large objectives by breaking them down into smaller, more manageable tasks. This concept can be applied to real life as well. When faced with a significant goal, dissect it into small, actionable steps or tasks.

For instance, if your quest is to start a successful business, the tasks could include market research, creating a business plan, securing funding, and launching your product or service. By breaking down big goals into smaller tasks, you not only make them more achievable but also create a roadmap for progress.

Staying Motivated on Your Journey

In video games, motivation is often driven by the promise of rewards, the thrill of exploration, and the sense of accomplishment. To maintain motivation in your real-life quests, tap into these principles:

Rewards and Recognition

Reward yourself for completing milestones and achieving goals. This can be as simple as treating yourself to something you enjoy or acknowledging your accomplishments.

Visualize Success

Imagine the satisfaction of achieving your quests and the positive impact it will have on your life.

Visualization can be a powerful motivator.

Find Allies

Just as characters in games often have companions, seek out allies and supporters who can cheer you on and hold you accountable.

Celebrate Progress

Celebrate not only the completion of quests but also your progress along the way. Small wins build momentum.

Stay Curious

Embrace the curiosity of exploration. Approach your quests with a sense of wonder and a desire to learn and grow.

Setting goals and transforming them into quests is a fundamental skill for success in both gaming and real life. By adhering to the **SMART** criteria, gamifying your goals, breaking them down into manageable tasks, and staying motivated through rewards and recognition, you can turn your journey into an exciting adventure filled with progress and achievement. Just like a skilled gamer, you have the tools to navigate life's challenges and emerge victorious in your quests.

Goal Setting

In the gaming world and in life, setting clear and actionable goals is the foundation for progress and success. These pages will help you transform your aspirations into exciting quests, just like your favorite video game missions. Use this page to define your goals, break them down into manageable tasks, and maintain motivation throughout your journey.

Goal Title:

_____

Goal Description:

Describe your goal in detail. Be specific about what you want to achieve, why it's important to you, and how it aligns with your character's journey.

_____

_____

_____

Goal Type: (Select one or more)

- ○ Personal Growth

- ○ Career Advancement

- ○ Health and Fitness

- ○ Relationships

- ○ Financial

- ○ Education

- ○ Creative Pursuits

- ○ Other: _____

SMART Goals: (Specific, Measurable, Achievable, Relevant, Time-bound)

Specific:

What exactly do you want to accomplish?

_____

_____

Measurable:

How will you track your progress and determine when you've achieved this goal?

_____

_____

Achievable:

Is this goal realistic and attainable? Do you have the necessary resources and support?

_____

_____

Relevant:

How does this goal align with your character's journey and overall aspirations?

_____

_____

Time-bound:

When do you intend to achieve this goal? Set a target date for completion.

Goal
Deadline:_____

Milestones:

Break down your goal into small, manageable milestones or tasks. Milestones help you track your progress and celebrate achievements along the way.

Milestone 1:

_____

Deadline:_____

Milestone 2:

_____

Deadline:_____

Milestone 3:

_____

Deadline:_____

Motivation:

What motivates you to pursue this goal? Understanding your motivation can help you stay committed during challenges.

_____

_____

_____

_____

Obstacles and Solutions:

Anticipate potential obstacles or challenges that may arise on your quest to achieve this goal. Then, brainstorm possible solutions or strategies to overcome them.

Obstacle 1:

_____

Solution:

_____

Obstacle 2:

_____

Solution:

_____

Obstacle 3:

_____

Solution:

_____

Reward System:

Define rewards or incentives for achieving your milestones and ultimately your goal. Rewards can boost motivation and provide a sense of accomplishment.

Reward for Milestone 1:

_____

Reward for Milestone 2:

_____

Reward for Milestone 3:

_____

Commitment:

By signing below, you acknowledge your commitment to pursuing this goal with determination, resilience, and unwavering dedication.

Character's Signature:

_____

Date: _____

Your completed goal-setting pages serve as a roadmap for your real-life quests. It helps you clarify your objectives, stay motivated, and navigate the challenges ahead. Remember, just like in your favorite games, each goal is a unique adventure waiting to be conquered. Embrace the journey, celebrate your victories along the way, and level up in every aspect of your life!

Chapter 6
Unlocking Skills and Abilities

In the realm of video games, characters are constantly acquiring new skills and abilities to overcome challenges and become more formidable. The same principle applies to real life. Learning new skills and abilities can be the key to unlocking your full potential and achieving your goals. In this chapter, we'll unlock effective methods for learning and acquiring skills, just as your favorite game characters do, and how to allocate your "skill points" wisely for maximum growth.

The Quest for Knowledge and Skills

Much like in a game, your journey in real life is enriched by the acquisition of knowledge and skills. Here's how you can embark on your quest for new abilities.

1. Online Courses and Education

One of the most accessible ways to learn new skills is through online courses and education platforms. Whether you're interested in mastering a programming language, learning a musical instrument, or acquiring a new language, there are countless online resources available. Websites like Coursera, edX, and Khan Academy offer a wide range of courses taught by experts.

2. Mentorship and Apprenticeship

In the gaming world, characters often seek the guidance of mentors to hone their abilities. In real life, finding a mentor or entering into an apprenticeship can provide invaluable learning experiences. Mentors offer insights, knowledge, and guidance that can fast-track your skill development.

3. Self-Directed Practice

Practice is the backbone of skill acquisition. Dedicate time to regular, focused practice in your chosen skill. Just as gamers repeat actions and drills to improve their in-game abilities, you can refine your real-life skills through dedicated practice.

4. Books and Resources

Books, tutorials, and resources specific to your chosen skill can be powerful tools for learning. Explore literature, manuals, and online communities related to your area of interest. These resources often provide deep insights and tips for success.

5. Online Communities and Forums

Engaging with like-minded individuals in online communities and forums can be a great way to share knowledge and gain insights. These platforms allow you to connect with experts and enthusiasts who are passionate about the same skills or interests.

Allocating Skill Points Wisely

In video games, characters often have limited skill points to distribute among various abilities. Similarly, in real life, you have limited time and resources to allocate to learning and skill development. Here's how to allocate your "skill points" wisely.

1. Prioritize Based on Goals

Consider your long-term goals and prioritize skills that align with them. If your goal is to excel in a specific career, allocate more skill points to areas directly related to that field.

2. Balance Your Skill Tree

Avoid over-investing in a single skill at the expense of neglecting others. Just as a balanced skill tree in a game makes for a more versatile character, a well-rounded skill set can enhance your adaptability in real life.

3. Continual Learning

Allocate some skill points to the skill of learning itself. Develop the ability to acquire new knowledge and skills efficiently. This meta-skill will serve you well in all aspects of life.

4. Measure Progress

Track your skill development and measure your progress. Just as a character's stats improve with experience, your abilities will grow over time. Regularly assess your skills and set new milestones to strive for.

5. Stay Open to Upgrades

In gaming, characters often seek upgrades to enhance their abilities. Similarly, stay open to upgrading your skills by exploring advanced courses or seeking out more challenging projects and experiences.

Unleash Your Inner Gamer

Learning skills and abilities in real life can be just as exciting and rewarding as the adventures of your favorite game characters. By embracing online courses, mentorship, self-directed practice, and the wealth of resources available, you can acquire new skills and abilities that empower you to level up in various aspects of your life. Remember to allocate your skill points wisely, prioritize based on your goals, and continually measure your progress. With determination and a gamer's spirit, you can unlock your full potential and thrive in the real-life quest for knowledge and mastery.

Skills and Abilities

In both gaming and real life, acquiring new skills and abilities is essential for growth and progress. These pages will help you keep track of the skills you're learning and how you're allocating your skill points, just like a character in your favorite video game.

Current Level: _____

Skill Points Available: _____

Skills and Abilities:

List the skills and abilities you're currently working on or have already acquired. Assign a level to each skill to indicate your proficiency, and use the skill points available to allocate towards your chosen skills.

Skill/Ability: _____
(e.g., Coding)

Level: _____

Skill Points Allocated: _____

Skill/Ability: _____
(e.g., Public Speaking)

Level: _____

Skill Points Allocated: _____

Skill/Ability: _____
(e.g., Cooking)

Level: _____

Skill Points Allocated: _____

Skill/Ability: _____
(e.g., Negotiation)

Level: _____

Skill Points Allocated: _____

Skill/Ability: _____
(e.g., Graphic Design)
Level: _____

Skill Points Allocated: _____

Skill Progress:

Track your progress for each skill by noting specific achievements, milestones, or improvements related to that skill.

Skill Progress:

_____

_____

Skill Progress:

_____

_____

Skill Progress:

_____

_____

Skill Progress:

_____

_____

Skill Progress:

_____

_____

Skill Points Allocation:

Decide how you want to allocate your skill points to improve your character's abilities. Be strategic and consider the skills that will benefit your character's journey the most.

Skill Points Allocation Plan:

_____

Skill Points Allocation Plan:

_____

Skill Points Allocation Plan:

_____

Skill Points Allocation Plan:

_____

Skill Points Allocation Plan:

_____

Goals for Skill Development:

Set specific goals for each skill, including what level you aim to reach and any associated rewards or benefits.

Skill Development Goal:

_____

Skill Development Goal:

_____

Skill Development Goal:

_____

Skill Development Goal:

_____

Skill Development Goal:

_____

These Skills and Abilities pages will help you organize and track your real-life skill development, just like a character sheet in a video game. It allows you to set goals, allocate skill points strategically, and monitor your progress as you continue to level up in various aspects of your life.

Chapter 7
Facing Challenges and
Boss Battles

Life is an epic journey filled with challenges and, occasionally, "boss battles" that test our mettle and determination. Much like in your favorite video games, these formidable foes can be overcome with the right mindset, strategies, and support network. In this chapter, we'll dive into how to approach life's challenges and boss battles with confidence, resilience, and the power of teamwork.

The Nature of Life's Challenges

Just as in video games, life's challenges come in various forms. Some are minor obstacles, akin to low-level enemies, while others are major trials that resemble daunting boss battles. Understanding the nature of these challenges is the first step in conquering them.

1. Identify the Challenge

Begin by identifying the specific challenge you're facing. What is the nature of the obstacle? Is it a personal setback, a professional hurdle, or a health-related concern? Define the challenge clearly to strategize effectively.

2. Analyze Your Resources

Like a gamer assessing their inventory and abilities before a boss fight, evaluate your resources. What skills, knowledge, and support systems can you tap into to overcome this challenge?

3. Develop a Strategy

Approach each challenge with a well-thought-out strategy. Break down the problem into small, manageable steps, much like tackling different phases of a boss battle. Consider the potential risks and rewards of each action.

4. Seek Guidance

Just as video game characters often receive guidance from mentors or allies, seek advice and guidance from those who have faced similar challenges. Their insights and experience can be invaluable.

5. Embrace Adaptability

In both life and gaming, adaptability is a key factor in success. Plan for contingencies, and be willing to switch tactics if the situation demands it. Flexibility and resilience are vital in the face of unexpected twists.

Building Your Support Network

Facing life's challenges alone can be daunting, much like going into a boss battle solo. Building a support network of allies, friends, and mentors can provide the encouragement and assistance you need.

1. Lean on Friends and Family

Your loved ones are often your most reliable allies. Share your challenges with them, and don't hesitate to ask for their support and advice.

2. Seek Professional Guidance

Just as characters in games consult experts for advice, consider seeking professional help when needed. Therapists, coaches, and counselors can provide guidance for personal and mental health challenges.

3. Join Supportive Communities

Online and offline communities offer a sense of belonging and shared experiences. Seek out groups and communities related to your specific challenge, and connect with individuals who understand what you're going through.

4. Collaborate with Allies

In video games, characters often form parties to take on challenging foes. In real life, collaborate with others who have complementary skills or expertise. Teamwork can provide new perspectives and solutions.

5. Give and Receive Help

Just as you may offer help to other gamers in multiplayer games, be open to giving and receiving help within your support network. Building a reciprocal relationship with others strengthens your bonds.

Maintaining Resilience and Determination

Boss battles in video games can be grueling, requiring persistence and determination to overcome. Similarly, facing life's challenges demands unwavering resilience and determination.

1. Stay Positive

Maintain a positive outlook even in the face of adversity. A positive mindset can help you navigate challenges more effectively and bounce back from setbacks.

2. Celebrate Small Wins

Just as characters celebrate minor victories in games, celebrate your small wins along the way. These milestones can fuel your determination and motivation.

3. Reflect and Learn

After overcoming a challenge, take time to reflect on the experience. What did you learn? How can you apply these lessons to future challenges?

4. Embrace the Journey

Life's challenges are an integral part of your personal growth journey, much like boss battles are integral to a game's storyline. Embrace the journey, and view challenges as opportunities for growth and self-discovery.

Conquer Your Boss Battles

In the game of life, challenges and boss battles are inevitable. However, with the right mindset, strategies, and support network, you have the tools to conquer them. Approach each challenge with confidence, adaptability, and a well-thought-out strategy. Build a strong support network of allies and mentors to aid you on your journey. Maintain resilience and determination, and remember that every boss battle you overcome brings you one step closer to achieving your ultimate objectives in the grand adventure of life.

Battle Strategy

Facing challenges and "boss battles" in real life requires a well-thought-out strategy, just like in your favorite video games. These pages will help you plan your approach to formidable foes, problems, or obstacles you encounter in your journey.

Current Challenge/Boss Battle:

_____

Challenge Description:

Describe the challenge or obstacle you're currently facing. Be specific about its nature, significance, and potential impact on your character's journey.

_____

_____

Allies and Supporters:

List the allies, supporters, or individuals who can assist you in overcoming this challenge. Allies can provide valuable perspectives, expertise, or support.

Ally/Supporter 1:

_____

Role/Expertise:

_____

Ally/Supporter 2:

_____

Role/Expertise:

_____

Ally/Supporter 3:

_____

Role/Expertise:

_____

Enemy or Challenge Weaknesses:

Identify any weaknesses or vulnerabilities in the challenge or obstacle you're facing. Understanding its weaknesses can help you strategize effectively.

Weakness 1:

_____

Weakness 2:

_____

Weakness 3:

_____

Battle Strategy:

Outline your battle strategy for overcoming this challenge. Consider the strengths of your character and allies, as well as the weaknesses of the challenge. Be specific about the steps you'll take.

Strategy Step 1:

_____

Strategy Step 2:

_____

Strategy Step 3:

_____

Strategy Step 4:

_____

Strategy Step 5:

_____

Contingency Plan:

Prepare for unexpected twists or obstacles that may arise during the battle. What backup plans or alternative strategies will you have in place?

Contingency Plan:

_____

Contingency Plan:

_____

Contingency Plan:

_____

Progress Tracking:

Use this section to monitor your progress as you implement your battle strategy. Record achievements, milestones, or setbacks related to this challenge.

Progress Update:

_____

Progress Update:

_____

Progress Update:

_____

Reflection and Learning:

After overcoming the challenge, reflect on what you've learned and how it has contributed to your character's growth and journey.

Reflection:

_____

_____

_____

_____

_____

These Battle Strategy pages are your guide to facing challenges and "boss battles" in real life with a clear plan of action. By outlining your strategy, considering allies and weaknesses, and preparing for contingencies, you'll be better equipped to overcome formidable foes on your journey to leveling up in the real world.

Chapter 8
Leveling Up Your Health and Well-being

In both the gaming world and real life, a character's health and well-being play a pivotal role in their success. Your real-life journey is no different, and taking care of your physical and mental health is essential for achieving your goals and enjoying a fulfilling life. In this chapter, we'll explore strategies for leveling up your health and well-being, including exercise, nutrition, stress management, and the transformative power of meditation and mindfulness.

The Vital Importance of Health and Well-being

Just as in video games, where a character's health bar determines their resilience and ability to face challenges, your physical and mental well-being impact your ability to navigate life's obstacles and triumph over them.

1. Physical Health

Physical health encompasses your overall physical fitness, strength, and vitality. It affects your energy levels, endurance, and ability to take on the demands of daily life.

2. Mental Health

Mental health involves your emotional well-being, cognitive function, and psychological resilience. A healthy mind is better equipped to handle stress, make decisions, and maintain a positive outlook.

Strategies for Physical Health

1. Regular Exercise

Exercise is the cornerstone of physical health. Incorporate regular physical activity into your routine, whether it's through daily walks, jogging, strength training, or engaging in sports. Exercise not only improves your physical fitness but also releases endorphins, enhancing your mood.

2. Balanced Nutrition

Just as characters in games need nourishment to sustain themselves, your body requires proper nutrition. Prioritize a well-rounded eating plan that includes plenty of fruits, vegetables, lean proteins, and whole grains. Limit the intake of processed foods and sugars.

3. Quality Sleep

Restorative sleep is essential for physical and mental well-being. Prioritize sleep hygiene practices, such as maintaining a regular sleep schedule, creating a comfortable sleep environment, and limiting screen time before bedtime.

4. Regular Health Check-ups

Regular medical check-ups and screenings are crucial for detecting and addressing health issues early. Don't neglect preventive healthcare; it's an investment in your long-term well-being.

Strategies for Mental Health

1. Stress Management

Develop effective stress management techniques, such as mindfulness meditation, deep breathing exercises, or yoga. These practices can help reduce stress and anxiety, improving your mental health.

2. Seek Support

Just as characters often rely on allies for assistance, don't hesitate to seek support from friends, family, or mental health professionals when facing emotional challenges. Talking to someone you trust can provide valuable perspective and emotional relief.

3. Self-Care

Prioritize self-care practices, such as engaging in hobbies, taking breaks, and setting boundaries. Self-care is not a luxury but a necessity for maintaining mental well-being.

4. Lifelong Learning

Engaging in continuous learning and mental stimulation, such as reading, puzzles, or pursuing new skills, keeps your mind sharp and adaptable.

Harnessing the Power of Meditation and Mindfulness

Meditation and mindfulness practices offer profound benefits for both physical and mental well-being. They provide tools for self-awareness, stress reduction, and emotional regulation.

1. Mindfulness Meditation

Mindfulness meditation entails cultivating a state of complete presence, where you observe your thoughts and sensations without any judgment or attachment to them. Regular practice can enhance your ability to manage stress and maintain a calm and centered mind.

2. Guided Meditation

Guided meditation sessions, often available through apps and online resources, can assist you in developing mindfulness and relaxation skills. These sessions are particularly helpful for beginners.

3. Yoga and Tai Chi

Practices like yoga and Tai Chi combine physical exercise with mindfulness techniques, promoting both flexibility and mental clarity. These disciplines are excellent for holistic well-being.

A Healthier, Happier You

Just as a gamer ensures their character's health and well-being to succeed in the game, prioritizing your physical and mental health is essential for achieving success and fulfillment in real life. By incorporating regular exercise, balanced nutrition, stress management, and mindfulness practices into your daily routine, you can level up your health and well-being. Remember that a healthier, happier you is better equipped to conquer life's challenges, achieve your goals, and savor the journey along the way.

Health and Well-being Goals

Just like in your favorite video games, maintaining your character's health and well-being is crucial in real life. These pages will help you strategize and track your efforts to enhance your physical and mental well-being, ensuring you're at your best for the challenges ahead.

Current Health and Well-being Level:

_____

Character's Health Bar: (Color in the number of blocks representing your current well-being level, with 10 blocks being the maximum)

Physical Health:

Exercise Routine:

Describe your current exercise routine, including types of exercises, frequency, and duration.

_____

_____

Nutrition:

Outline your dietary habits and any changes you'd like to make to improve your nutrition.

_____

_____

Sleep Quality:

Describe your sleep patterns and any strategies you use to ensure restful sleep.

_____

Mental Health:

Stress Management:

Explain how you manage and cope with stress in your daily life.

Mindfulness and Meditation:

Share your mindfulness or meditation practices and their impact on your mental well-being.

Hobbies and Relaxation:

List activities or hobbies that help you relax and recharge.

_____

_____

Character Abilities Unlocked:

What abilities or skills have you unlocked or enhanced by prioritizing your health and well-being? This could include increased energy, improved focus, or enhanced resilience.

Ability/Skill:

_____

Ability/Skill:

_____

Health and Well-being Goals:

Set specific goals for improving your physical and mental well-being. Consider what actions or changes will help you level up your character's health.

Health and Well-being Goal 1:

_____

_____

Health and Well-being Goal 2:

_____

_____

Health and Well-being Goal 3:

_____

_____

Progress Tracking:

Monitor your progress toward your health and well-being goals. Record achievements, milestones, or challenges you've encountered.

Progress Update:

_____

_____

Progress Update:

_____

_____

Progress Update:

_____

_____

Character's Reflection:

Reflect on the importance of maintaining your character's health and well-being and how it contributes to your overall journey and success.

Reflection:

_____

_____

_____

_____

_____

These Health and Well-being pages are your tool for prioritizing and enhancing your physical and mental well-being, just as you would manage your character's health in a video game. By setting goals, tracking progress, and reflecting on the impact of your efforts, you can ensure your character is at their best to tackle life's challenges and continue leveling up.

Recipes for Health Potions and Stamina-Restoring Meals

In the world of gaming, health potions and stamina-restoring items are essential for keeping your character in peak condition during epic quests and battles. Just as your favorite game characters rely on these concoctions for vitality and endurance, you too can benefit from real-life recipes that boost your health and stamina. In this chapter, we'll explore some delicious and nutritious recipes for homemade health potions (drinks) and meals that will help you maintain your well-being and energy levels.

Disclaimer:
The healthy recipes featured in this book are provided for informational and educational purposes only. They are not intended as medical advice or as a substitute for professional dietary guidance. Individual dietary needs and preferences may vary, and it is essential to consult with a qualified healthcare provider or nutritionist for personalized dietary recommendations, especially if you have specific health concerns or dietary restrictions.

These recipes are meant to promote a balanced and health-conscious approach to eating but should not be considered a replacement for personalized dietary assessments or medical recommendations. By using these recipes, you acknowledge and accept the terms of this disclaimer.

Health Potion Recipes

1.Elixir of Vitality

2.Herbal Infusion

1. Elixir of Vitality

Ingredients:

- 1 cup of fresh mixed berries (e.g., strawberries, blueberries, raspberries)
- 1/2 cup of Greek yogurt
- 1 tablespoon of honey
- 1/2 cup of almond milk
- 1/2 teaspoon of vanilla extract
- A pinch of cinnamon

Instructions:

1. Combine all the ingredients in a blender.

2. Blend until smooth.

3. Pour into a glass and enjoy this antioxidant-rich elixir for a health boost.

2. Herbal Infusion

Ingredients:

- 1 cup of hot water
- 1 tablespoon of fresh mint leaves (or tea leaves of your choice)
- 1 slice of lemon
- 1 teaspoon of honey (optional)

Instructions:

1. Place the mint leaves and lemon slice in a cup.

2. Pour hot water over them and let steep for a few minutes.

3. Add honey if desired.

4. Sip this soothing herbal infusion to refresh your body and mind.

Stamina-Restoring Meal Recipes

1.Power Packed Oatmeal

2.Grilled Chicken Salad

1. Power Packed Oatmeal

Ingredients:

- 1/2 cup of rolled oats
- 1 cup of almond milk
- 1 banana, sliced
- 1 tablespoon of almond butter
- 1 tablespoon of chia seeds
- A sprinkle of cinnamon

Instructions:

1. Cook the oats in almond milk until creamy.

2. Top with banana slices, almond butter, chia seeds, and a sprinkle of cinnamon.

3. This nutrient-rich oatmeal will replenish your energy and keep you full for hours.

2. Grilled Chicken Salad

Ingredients:

- 4 oz grilled chicken breast, sliced
- 1 cup of mixed greens (e.g., spinach, kale, arugula)
- 1/4 cup of cherry tomatoes, halved
- 1/4 cup of onion, diced
- 1/4 cup of avocado, sliced

Instructions:

1. In a bowl, combine the grilled chicken, mixed greens, cherry tomatoes, onion, and avocado.

2. Drizzle with balsamic vinaigrette and toss to coat.

3. This protein-packed salad is perfect for refueling after a long day.

Just as in your favorite video games, maintaining health and stamina is vital for success in real life. These recipes for homemade health potions and stamina-restoring meals will help you stay energized, focused, and ready to take on any challenge. Incorporate these nutritious and delicious options into your daily routine to level up your well-being and endurance. It's a culinary adventure!

Chapter 9
Social Interaction and Networking

In both the gaming world and real life, forming alliances and building relationships can be the key to success. Your ability to interact effectively with others, network, and collaborate can significantly impact your personal and professional journey. In this chapter, we'll explore strategies for improving your social skills, networking effectively, and creating a party of like-minded individuals to tackle life's challenges together.

The Power of Social Interaction

Just as in video games, where characters often form parties to overcome formidable foes and accomplish quests, your interactions with others can enhance your capabilities and help you achieve your goals in real life.

1. Improving Social Skills

Effective social interaction begins with strong social skills. Whether you're an introvert or an extrovert, honing your ability to communicate, empathize, and connect with others is essential.

2. Networking Effectively

Networking involves building a network of contacts and allies who can support your goals and provide valuable insights and opportunities.

3. Collaboration and Teamwork

Collaboration is about working together with others to achieve a common goal. It requires effective communication, cooperation, and mutual respect.

Strategies for Social Interaction and Networking

1. Actively Listen

Listening is a fundamental skill in effective communication. Develop the skill of active listening through the act of dedicating your complete focus to the speaker, seeking clarification where necessary, and demonstrating sincere curiosity regarding their viewpoint.

2. Develop Empathy

Empathy is a special ability that allows you to step into someone else's shoes and understand how they feel. Cultivate empathy by trying to see situations from another person's point of view. Empathy fosters deeper connections and smoother interactions.

3. Communication Skills

Enhance your communication skills by practicing clear and concise expression. Pay attention to nonverbal cues, such as body language and tone of voice, to convey your message effectively.

4. Expand Your Network

Seek out opportunities to expand your network. Attend professional and social events, join online communities, and participate in networking groups related to your interests and goals.

5. Nurture Relationships

Building and maintaining relationships takes effort. Stay in touch with contacts, express gratitude for their support, and offer help when you can. Authentic relationships are built on reciprocity and trust.

6. Collaborative Mindset

Approach collaboration with a cooperative mindset. Value the contributions of each team member and be open to diverse perspectives and ideas.

7. Set Clear Goals

In both networking and collaboration, setting clear goals is crucial. Define what you hope to achieve through your interactions, whether it's finding a mentor, securing a job opportunity, or completing a project.

Building Your Party of Allies

Just as characters in games assemble a party of allies with complementary skills and abilities, you can create a network of individuals who share your goals and values. This "party" can be a valuable asset in overcoming challenges and achieving success.

1. Identify Like-Minded Individuals

Seek out individuals who share your interests, ambitions, and values. These like-minded individuals are more likely to become valuable allies in your journey.

2. Diverse Perspectives

While like-mindedness is important, also value diversity of thought and experience. A diverse group of allies can offer fresh perspectives and creative solutions to challenges.

3. Define Roles and Responsibilities

Just as characters in a party have distinct roles and abilities, clarify the roles and responsibilities of your allies within the group. Ensure that each member brings something unique to the table.

4. Mutual Support

Foster a culture of mutual support and cooperation within your party. Encourage members to assist each other in achieving their individual and collective goals.

5. Adaptability

Life's challenges may require different approaches and strategies. Be adaptable and open to adjusting your party's tactics as needed.

Forge Strong Alliances

In the grand adventure of life, forging strong alliances and mastering the art of social interaction and networking can significantly impact your success and happiness. By developing your social skills, networking effectively, and collaborating with others, you can assemble a party of allies who share your goals and values. Together, you can overcome challenges, achieve your objectives, and savor the camaraderie of the journey.

Social Interaction and Networking Goals

In both gaming and real life, building relationships and alliances can be the key to success. These pages will help you strategize, track your social interactions, and plan your networking efforts to achieve your goals.

Current Level of Social Interaction and Networking:

_____

Character's Social Circle: (Color in the number of blocks representing your current social interaction level, with 10 blocks being the maximum)

Social Interaction and Networking Goals:

Define specific goals for improving your social interaction and networking skills. Consider what connections and relationships will benefit your character's journey.

Social Goal 1:

_____

_____

Social Goal 2:

_____

_____

Social Goal 3:

_____

_____

Networking Strategies:

Outline your strategies for expanding your network and building valuable connections. Describe the methods you plan to use to enhance your networking abilities.

Networking Strategy 1:

_____

_____

Networking Strategy 2:

_____

_____

Networking Strategy 3:

_____

_____

Current Connections and Allies:

List individuals or groups with whom you already have a connection or alliance. Include their roles or areas of expertise.

Connection/Ally 1:

_____

Role/Expertise:

_____

Connection/Ally 2:

_____

Role/Expertise:

_____

Connection/Ally 3:

_____

Role/Expertise:

_____

Content:

Networking Achievements:

Record achievements related to your networking efforts. This could include forming new connections, receiving mentorship, or collaborating on projects.

Achievement 1:

_____

_____

Achievement 2:

_____

_____

Achievement 3:

_____

_____

Party Building:

In gaming, parties or teams are essential for tackling challenges. Describe how you plan to build or strengthen your "party" of like-minded individuals who can help you achieve your goals.

Party Building Plan:

_____

_____

_____

_____

Social Interaction Progress:

Use this section to monitor your progress in enhancing your social interaction and networking skills. Record achievements, milestones, or challenges you've encountered.

Progress Update:

_____

_____

Progress Update:

_____

_____

Progress Update:

_____

_____

Character's Reflection:

Reflect on the importance of social interaction and networking in your character's journey and how it contributes to your overall success.

Reflection:

_____

_____

_____

_____

_____

These Social Interaction and Networking pages will guide you in expanding your social circle, forming valuable connections, and building alliances just as you would in your favorite video games. By setting goals, planning networking strategies, and tracking your progress, you can enhance your character's social interaction and networking abilities to tackle challenges and achieve your goals in real life.

Chapter 10
Staying Engaged and Avoiding Burnout

Gaming teaches us that long-term enjoyment is often more rewarding than quick wins. In real life, maintaining engagement and avoiding burnout are essential for sustained success and happiness. In this chapter, we'll explore techniques for staying engaged in your pursuits, striking a balance, setting boundaries, and recognizing when to take well-deserved breaks to recharge.

The Pitfalls of Burnout

In both gaming and real life, burnout can be a formidable adversary. It occurs when prolonged stress and exhaustion sap your energy, motivation, and enthusiasm. Avoiding burnout is crucial for maintaining your well-being and achieving your long-term goals.

1. Finding Balance

Achieving balance in your life is akin to leveling up your character in a game. Balance means allocating time and energy to various aspects of your life, including work, personal pursuits, relationships, and self-care.

2. Setting Boundaries

Just as characters in games establish boundaries to protect their territory, you must set boundaries to safeguard your physical and mental health. Define what is acceptable and what isn't in terms of your commitments, work hours, and personal space.

3. Recognizing Signs of Burnout

Awareness is key to avoiding burnout. Be vigilant for signs of exhaustion, irritability, decreased motivation, and physical symptoms like headaches or sleep disturbances. Recognizing these signs early allows you to take action.

Strategies for Staying Engaged and Avoiding Burnout

1. Pursue Your Passions

Engagement thrives when you're passionate about your pursuits. Invest time in activities and projects that genuinely excite and interest you. Just as gamers revel in their favorite games, immerse yourself in what you love.

2. Practice Self-Care

Self-care is not a luxury but a necessity for maintaining well-being. Prioritize self-care practices, such as exercise, relaxation, hobbies, and spending quality time with loved ones.

3. Set Realistic Goals

In gaming, success often comes from setting achievable objectives and leveling up gradually. In real life, set realistic goals that challenge you but are attainable. This reduces the risk of burnout from pursuing unattainable ambitions.

4. Establish Work-Life Balance

Strive for a healthy work-life balance. Dedicate time to work, but also allocate time for relaxation, recreation, and personal growth. Avoid overextending yourself or neglecting your personal life for the sake of professional success.

5. Take Regular Breaks

In gaming, players take breaks to recharge and avoid

burnout during marathon sessions. Apply the same principle in real life. Take short breaks throughout your day to reset and recharge, and plan regular vacations to disconnect and rejuvenate.

6. Learn to Say No

Saying no when necessary is a skill that can protect you from overcommitting and burnout. Politely decline requests or commitments that may push you beyond your limits.

7. Seek Support and Perspective

Just as gamers seek advice and assistance from allies, don't hesitate to seek support or guidance from friends, family, or mentors when you're feeling overwhelmed. They can offer valuable perspective and solutions.

Embrace Long-Term Enjoyment

In the world of gaming, long-term enjoyment often stems from the joy of the journey itself, not just the destination. In real life, too, staying engaged and avoiding burnout is crucial for achieving sustained success and fulfillment. By finding balance, setting boundaries, recognizing signs of burnout, and practicing self-care, you can embrace long-term enjoyment in your pursuits. Remember that the key to a fulfilling life lies in navigating it with endurance and enthusiasm, just as a dedicated gamer does in their favorite game.

Staying Engaged and Avoiding Burnout Goals

In the world of gaming, long-term enjoyment and sustainability are key. These pages will help you strategize, track your engagement, and prevent burnout in your real-life adventures.

Current Level of Engagement: _____

Character's Engagement Meter: (Color in the number of blocks representing your current level of engagement, with 10 blocks being the maximum)

Current Challenges and Activities:

List the challenges or activities you're currently engaged in. These can include work, hobbies, personal projects, or any other endeavors.

Challenge/Activity 1:

_____

_____

Challenge/Activity 2:

_____

_____

Challenge/Activity 3:

_____

_____

Engagement Strategies:

Outline your strategies for staying engaged and motivated in your ongoing challenges and activities. Consider how you can maintain enthusiasm and prevent burnout.

Engagement Strategy 1:

_____

_____

Engagement Strategy 2:

_____

_____

Engagement Strategy 3:

_____

_____

Burnout Prevention:

Describe your methods for preventing burnout and maintaining balance in your life. What steps will you take to ensure long-term enjoyment?

Burnout Prevention Method 1:

_____

_____

Burnout Prevention Method 2:

_____

_____

Burnout Prevention Method 3:

_____

_____

Achievements and Milestones:

Record achievements and milestones related to your challenges and activities. Celebrate your progress to boost motivation.

Achievement/Milestone 1:

_____

_____

Achievement/Milestone 2:

_____

_____

Achievement/Milestone 3:

_____

_____

Time for Reflection:

Take time to reflect on your character's engagement and strategies for preventing burnout. Consider how maintaining balance contributes to your overall success.

Reflection:

_____

_____

_____

_____

_____

These Staying Engaged and Avoiding Burnout pages are your tool for sustaining long-term engagement and enjoyment in your real-life adventures, just as you would in gaming. By setting strategies, tracking your progress, and preventing burnout, you can ensure that your character remains enthusiastic and ready to tackle challenges on your journey.

Chapter 11
The End Game

In the world of gaming, reaching the "end game" is the ultimate goal—an achievement that signifies mastery, accomplishment, and the culmination of countless efforts. In real life, defining what success means to you and navigating the "end game" is just as important for a fulfilling and ever-evolving life. In this chapter, we'll discover how to set new challenges, continue leveling up, and create a life that remains fulfilling and ever-evolving.

Defining Success on Your Terms

Success is all about personal perspective and can mean different things to different people. Before you embark on your journey to the "end game," take the time to define what success means to you. Is it a specific career achievement, financial security, a happy family, personal growth, or something else entirely? Knowing your definition of success will guide your efforts and provide clarity on your goals.

1. Reflect on Your Values

Consider what values are most important to you. Is it creativity, adventure, stability, freedom, or something else? Aligning your goals with your core values is essential for a meaningful end game.

2. Set Milestones

Success is often a journey with milestones along the way. Break down your long-term goals into smaller, more achievable milestones. Celebrate these achievements as you progress toward your ultimate vision of success.

3. Stay Open to Evolution

As you approach your initial goals, remain open to the possibility that your definition of success may evolve. Life experiences and personal growth can lead you in new directions. Be willing to adapt your goals accordingly.

Continuing to Level Up

In gaming, reaching the "end game" often doesn't mean the adventure is over; instead, it's a new beginning. Similarly, in real life, reaching your initial goals can be a stepping stone to new challenges and opportunities. Here's how to continue leveling up:

1. Embrace Lifelong Learning

The quest for knowledge and personal growth never ends. Continue to learn, explore, and develop new skills and abilities. The more you learn, the more you can contribute to your own success and the world around you.

2. Set New Challenges

Once you've achieved your initial goals, set new challenges that align with your evolving definition of success. These challenges should inspire and motivate you to keep growing and evolving.

3. Give Back and Make an Impact

Consider how you can use your skills and resources to make a positive impact on others and the world. Giving back and helping others is a fulfilling way to continue leveling up in life.

4. Cultivate Resilience

Being resilient means you can come back strong after tough times and things not going your way. Embrace challenges as opportunities for growth, and develop the resilience to overcome obstacles on your path to an ever-evolving life.

5. Enjoy the Journey

Remember that the journey itself is an integral part of the end game. Enjoy the process of striving toward your goals, savor the small wins, and find fulfillment in the everyday moments.

Creating an Ever-Evolving Life

An ever-evolving life is one where you're continuously adapting, learning, and growing, even after achieving initial success. It's about finding purpose and meaning in your journey rather than reaching a static destination.

1. Stay Curious

Approach life with curiosity and a thirst for knowledge. Cultivate a sense of wonder, and remain open to new experiences and opportunities.

2. Seek Balance

Maintain a balance between work, personal life, and self-care. Balance allows you to stay resilient and adaptable in the face of change.

3. Reevaluate Your Goals

Regularly reassess your goals and your definition of success. Make adjustments as needed to ensure they continue to align with your values and aspirations.

4. Celebrate Your Achievements

Celebrate not only the big milestones but also the small victories along the way. Acknowledge your progress and find joy in your accomplishments.

The Ever-Evolving Journey

The "end game" in life is not a static endpoint but a dynamic, ever-evolving journey of growth, learning, and fulfillment. Define success on your own terms, set new challenges, and continue leveling up in your pursuit of an ever-evolving life. Embrace the adventure, savor the moments, and relish the sense of achievement that comes from living a life that remains dynamic and meaningful, just like your favorite game with endless quests and possibilities.

End Game Goals

Every gamer knows that reaching the "end game" is the ultimate goal. These pages will help you define what success means to you, set new challenges, and create a fulfilling and ever-evolving life.

Success Level: _____

Character's End Game Vision:

Describe your vision of success, what it looks like, and what achievements or milestones represent your "end game" in the grand adventure of life.

_____

_____

_____

_____

New Challenges and Quests:

Even after achieving your initial goals, life continues to offer new challenges and quests. List the new challenges or areas you'd like to explore in your ongoing journey.

New Challenge/Quest 1:

_____

_____

New Challenge/Quest 2:

_____

_____

New Challenge/Quest 3:

_____

_____

Leveling Up Your Character:

Outline how you plan to continue leveling up and evolving as a character. Consider skills to develop, areas for growth, and opportunities to expand your horizons.

Character Development Goal 1:

_____

_____

Character Development Goal 2:

_____

_____

Character Development Goal 3:

_____

_____

Personal Legacy:

Think about the legacy you want to leave behind. How do you want to be remembered, and what impact do you want to make on the world?

Personal Legacy:

_____

_____

_____

Game Continues:

Remember, life is an ongoing game. Embrace the idea that your character's journey is ever-evolving, and new adventures await.

Character's Commitment to Continued Growth:

_____

_____

_____

_____

Reflection and Celebration:

Reflect on your character's journey, the challenges you've overcome, and the progress you've made. Celebrate your achievements and look forward to the exciting chapters ahead.

Reflection:

_____

_____

_____

_____

_____

These End Game pages encourage you to define your vision of success, set new challenges, and embrace the concept of an ever-evolving journey. By continuously leveling up, striving for personal growth, and leaving a positive legacy, you can create a fulfilling and dynamic life beyond your initial goals.

Conclusion

"Life XP: Unlocking Achievements and Leveling Up in the Real World" has been your companion on a remarkable journey, a journey that transcends the virtual and bridges the gap between the digital and real worlds. Throughout this guide, you've uncovered the invaluable wisdom and strategies inspired by the world of gaming, all tailored to help you thrive and succeed in the reality you inhabit.

As you close this chapter of your adventure, remember that the principles you've embraced here are not confined to the confines of a screen or the pixels of a game. They are the tools that empower you to embark on a quest of self-discovery and personal growth. Whether you're striving for personal excellence, advancing in your career, or simply seeking a more fulfilling life, this guide has equipped you to navigate the challenges and opportunities that lie ahead.

In your hands, you hold the blueprint for leveling up in every aspect of your life. Just as a gamer relishes the thrill of a new quest and the satisfaction of achieving new levels of mastery, you too can approach life with the same enthusiasm and determination. Life itself is the ultimate game, and you possess the power to level up, overcome obstacles, and achieve greatness.

As you embark on the next chapter of your real-life adventure, remember these words: Game on! With the gamer's mindset, the drive to level up, and the wisdom you've gained from this guide, there are no limits to what you can achieve. Your journey is a tapestry of quests, challenges, and triumphs waiting to be woven, and the story you create is uniquely yours.

May your quests be fulfilling, your allies steadfast, and your achievements abundant as you continue to embrace the principles of gaming and level up in the grand adventure that is your life. Farewell, and may your path be filled with endless possibilities and boundless achievements.

Be sure to check out our Etsy store, LifeXP2024, where real life meets gaming vibes! Dive into a world of unique products inspired by Life XP: Unlocking Achievements and Leveling Up in the Real World. Level up your wardrobe with our stylish apparel, enhance your space with gaming-inspired home decor, and keep the adventure going with our range of accessories. Embrace the spirit of leveling up in real life with our one of a kind items. Come on in and start unlocking achievements in style!

https://www.etsy.com/shop/LifeXP2024?ref=profile_header